Preface

What is life, but a tale.

Chitrakathi (चित्रकथी) is a Sanskrit name for storytellers who narrate stories using the medium of words, songs, puppetry, paintings, and poetry.

These poems are voices of my emotions that tell stories of love, pain, hope, and desire.

At the expense of stating the obvious, this book is perhaps a subconscious ordeal of my ego, but it is also most certainly an earnest attempt at documenting a man's journey through life. I've tried my best not to fester these stories with the toxicity of chasing perfection, or soil them with post-adornment and rob them of their innocence. I've tried to preserve the naivety of a novice lover, the vulnerability of a mourning heart, the freshness of a newfound joy, and the depths of a pensive mind. It is a sneak peek into my personal diary, as an invitation to an opera of life experiences. It is also a requiem for those countless feelings that are often unheard, inaccessible, or even disowned.

This book is for you if you have ever been in love. It's for you if you have lost. If you have felt hopeless, and have been alone and confused. If you have felt at peace. If you have been nostalgic. If you have felt confident, and playful. If you have felt angry and hateful. If you have felt insignificant and small. If you have been rejected. It's for you if you have been taken for granted. If you have been abused. It's for you if you are looking for some company in your own quest to (re)find happiness.

I extend my gratitude to those who have been the inspiration behind this work, the people whom I met on my journey, including those who have had to say goodbye. Without them, I would neither have felt nor imagined any of this.

This book is a result of incentives I received from friends and family, and some strangers whom I fortuitously met in my travels. Who were curious and patient enough to lend me their ears. In particular, I wish to thank Abhishek, Paula, and Nina for their feedback and for convincing me to share this work with people outside my immediate circle of acquaintances. I thank Arnie for educating me on the tools of book publishing, and

Chitrakathi

Lord Nayak

चित्रकथी

लॉर्ड नायक

introducing me to the joys of book design. I thank Avi for dissolving my ego with his unyielding friendship. Finally, I thank my mum, who torched my insecurities with her words of wisdom and affection.

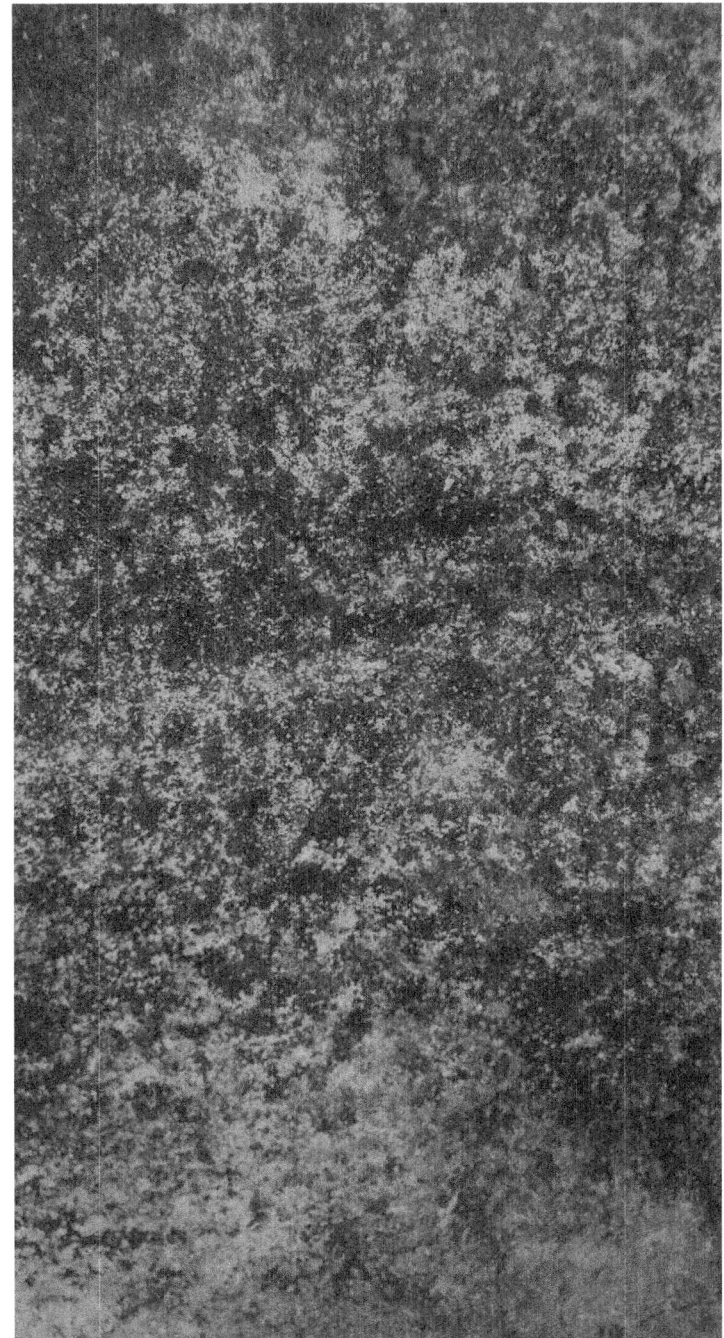

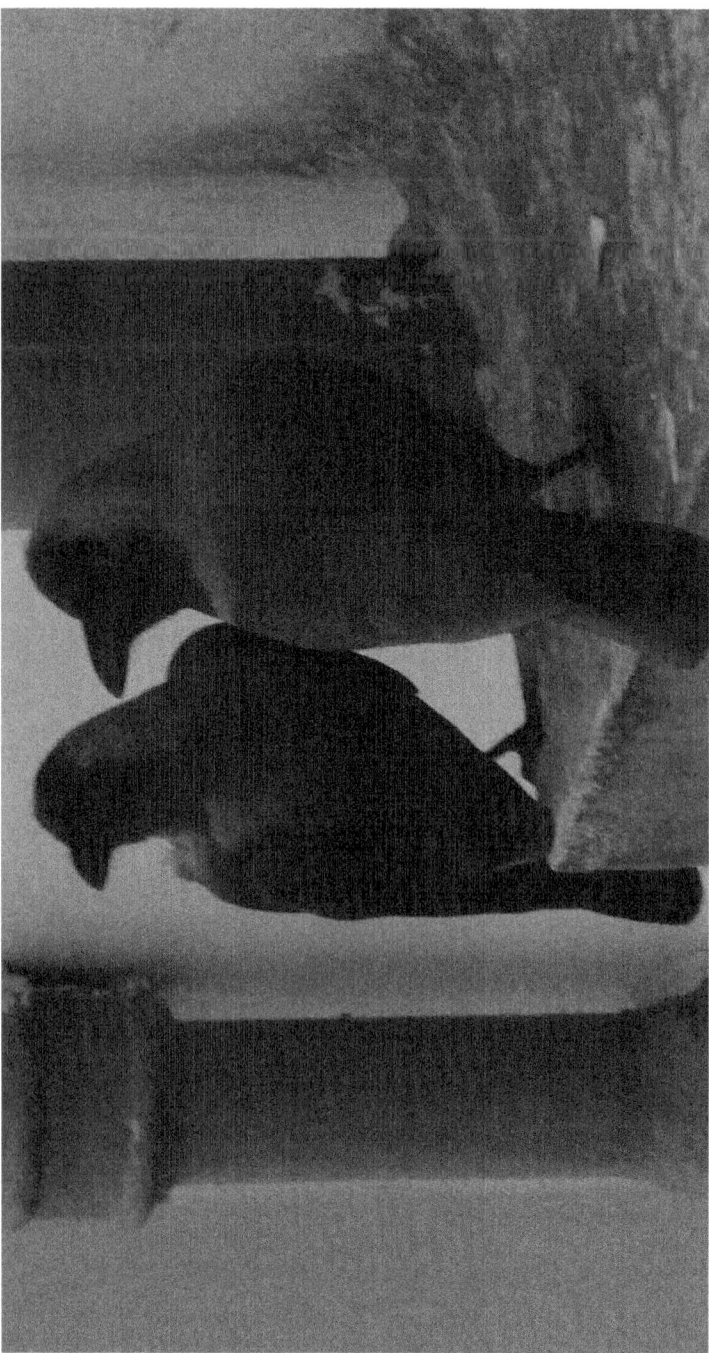

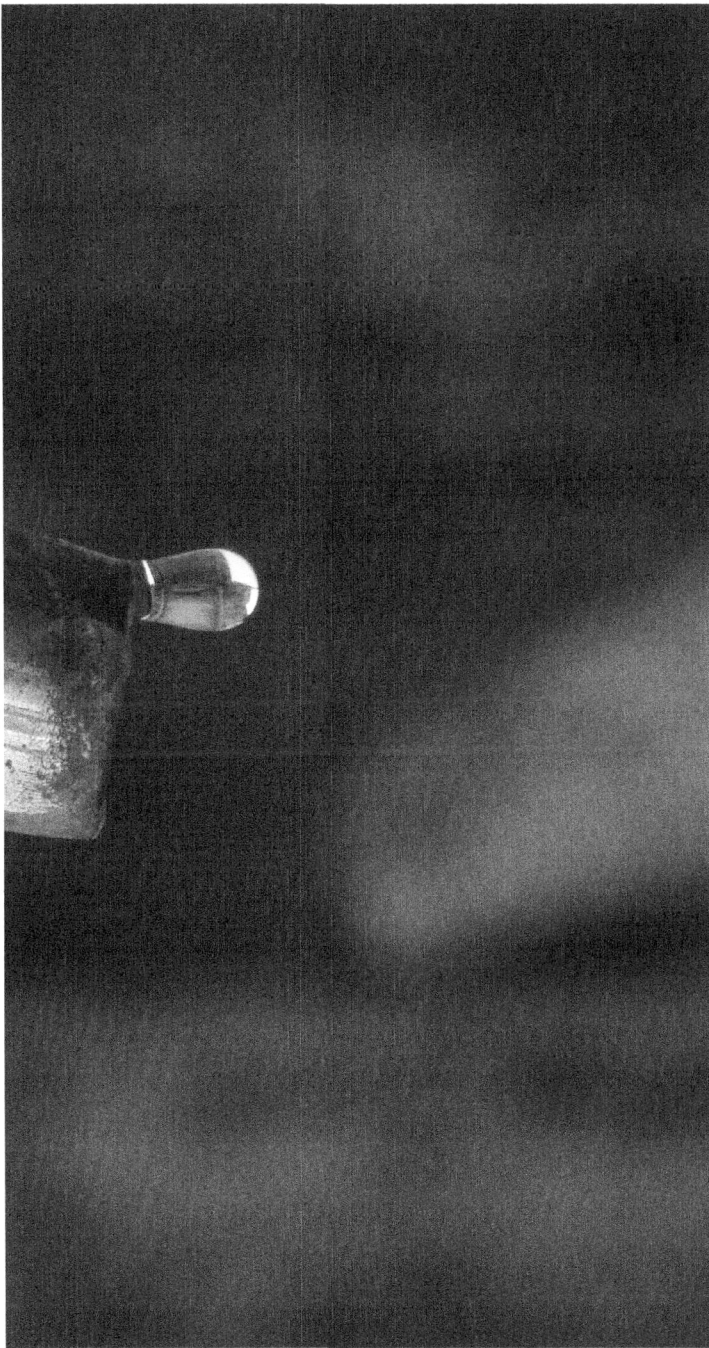

LOVE

How could you fall in love with me when you don't even
know who I'm, **she says**.

I don't know what's the diameter of the moon,
how many craters there are on it,
how far it is from our planet,
what's the composition of the soil on it,
what's there in its very core,
what lies on its darker side,
or if life would ever be possible on it.
Yet I fell in love with it the instance I saw it.
It's so special.
It's the only moon around the only living planet known to
the human kind.
Not even the sun can charm me for its bright light.
I just happen to love the moonlight.
And that when I see you I know that there goes the one
who carries with her my heart, and my last first kiss.

The maroons of twilight

In the hours of twilight
upon evening's plea,
with skies as blue
as crimson can be,
if words were whispered
were only vessels,
how shall perfect
a heart one see

Navy silhouettes
of hills and clouds,
scarf the pink
and red wrinkled blouse,
the scent of salt
and orange flames,
accent the song
of now weary waves

A play is afoot
chanced in display,
of swooping terns
and a slinking haar,
unfolding on
this purple stage,
are muddled wishes
and a riddled past

With shifting shapes
of picturesque folds
and merging shades
of lilac and gold
In guises of winds
and songs of sea
the maroons of twilight
are talking to me

PASSION

1/8/22

Twisted with turmoils of life the mind runs restless and yet all it takes is just an idea of existence of true love that turns the barren lands of despair into springs of hope and breezes of long deep breaths of fresh air.

So we have not met yet, yet your green scent is fresh in my memory, your warm touch is no stranger to my skin, and every so often I lose myself in your presence, that nurtures the flame in my finest of hopes that you find me before does death.

A prelude to a vision

The winds and the seasons
are poignant in despair
and the tree trails silently pine
for I no longer long to sway
in their rhythm and my songs
now belong to someone else

I spend my days in flight without feathers
musing on the vinous scent
of your plush fragrant skin
and run my hands
through the shallow rivers, and my face
under the waterfalls
to sense the flow of your long brown locks
that exude a jasmine savour

Your existence gives the sun and the moon
their purpose to scale the vastness of eternity
as they emerge in the heavens
to shine their light upon your iridescent face

Your mellow chromatic eyes are
deeper than galaxies, and house
a bright mesmerizing spark
that invite me to gaze upon your soul
and embrace your divine grace

Your lush pink lips are tulips and roses,
and are grails to the elixir of life itself
and your simple smile is a sacred promise
that I spent a lifetime searching for

For I've spent many moons in vain
chasing the light of fairytale fireflies
and as a wave I've rippled across the oceans
in search of my final shore
and now that I've seen you
my life, I deem complete

With every prayer whispered in the wind I gaze upon the doors locked ahead, and day by day I search for the face in the mirror that once travelled far and beyond, left within the confines of my own solitude, searching my dreams for your shadows. I don't wish for a lifetime of love, but I need to learn what it's like to love you completely even if just for a moment.

The love I seek, for its purity and absoluteness, inside the mist of illusion and darkness of which it's born, is bound to be mortal and short-lived. Its subtle soft taste that my imagination bears drives me erratic, as if I was suddenly pushed into an endless empty tunnel blindfolded but convinced of this enigmatic pulse of light.

In her face I sensed the rhythm of this scintillating white light which brought to life everything it touched, although oblivious to the infinite spectrum of colours hidden within. I wonder how life would have been if only I could have shown her the meaning of her being to myself.

While witnessing the wars of will and whims, pensive on the warm rough concrete edge of the garden seat, I sit overwhelmed with an inordinately gripping sense of need to fill the void that exists in her absence. It's a true tragedy: two longing souls strapped within the shackles of unworthy promises, caged in the confinements of world order, and lost in the illusion of stability.

All it takes is an honest heart for the blind to see, and muster the courage to indulge in the only reality of true love. If only it were to be granted as a last wish I would die without a doubt to let her see for herself the depths of my love for her.

A wastrel in love

A scent of flowers
haunts my closed eyes again,
the appetite
to see someone's face has returned,
the longing
for nonsensical talks is born again,
the craving
for slow intoxicating walks recur

The need to write songs to curb this crisis within
has turned the once busy hours into futile forms,
the once king who slept high up in closed castles
awaits now a life laden letter to arrive as a timekeeping
wastrel

I cherish the wait tending your arrival
as a sunflower at night,
this sweet pain is a cure
to the insomnia induced by an overwhelming and
numbing gale of emotions,
this intangible void is a comforting vessel
that holds my spirit now,
this state of mind is a tomb
to my soul now

If you were drowning
I would plunge without query into uncouth currents to
rescue you,
If I lost you to the depths of the wild sea
I would drink up all the oceans to be with you

I long to visit your birth place as a pilgrim
and study your past as theology
and serenade you in the hours of the day with my poems
that are prayers,
for worshiping you is my religion now

Your presence inspires poetry inside of me, that
spontaneously flows as words from my mouth when I
talk to you, fuelled by the passion that runs deep in my
veins.

To me you are the blinding light of the morning sun,
and I'm falling free in your gravity,
with fresh air choking my lungs,
losing my senses in the awe of your pristine shimmering

beauty.

Yet, it is unfair,
as I fail to muster enough courage
to behold your blushing face and claim my reward,
as I fear,
I would lose myself, my sanity, and my soul
in those inviting and shapeshifting twin hazel eyes of
yours.

I fear not death
but the thought of losing you,
for I may survive death
but not losing you.

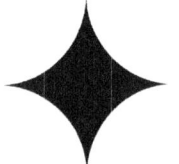

I sit in my 2nd floor flat waiting for her to come over, as we have planned to take our bikes on about a 30 km ride to North Berwick for a chippy, enjoying the beaches and the cycle trails on the way. It was quite warm that day. The weather she supposed would be raining in the morning, although I would later tell her that it was particularly dry for a rainy day.

On receiving her text that she's leaving her place, I opened my windows and positioned myself on the couch next to one of them from where I could just about see the reflections of people passing by my street on the windows of the cars parked in front of my lane. In particular, there was a street lamp where she would always park her bike before she came over to my flat, and I could see the pole of the lamp clearly from where I sat. I took my guitar out, and played some of my songs, transfixed on the reflection of that street lamp's pole on one of the car windows. As soon as I saw her reflection, my strumming became louder, just to hope that she hears a little bit of soothing music as she stood downstairs and rang my doorbell.

She looked particularly stunning that day. She had a light purple t-shirt on, that brought out the pinkness in her blushing supple cheeks, and provided a perfect base for her brown untied hair that embellished her back, over black denim shorts. I wanted to compliment her, and give her a kiss, but all I could do was go to the kitchen and fetch her a tumbler of cold tap water.

After cycling for about half an hour, we found a quiet golf course facing the sea, and thought it would be nice to sit there for a while, where she introduced me to pastel de nata - a Portuguese delicacy. I found it tasty, although my stomach made noises later as it was expecting more food. The pastry came in a dome-shaped aluminium cup to hold it. Sitting there I explained to her why such a spherical dome can not be transformed into a plane circle. The question was triggered by my indirect attempt to tell her how I felt about her, by asking how many different shapes could be made with that aluminium foil, as I quickly morphed mine into a heart-shaped figure.

Eventually, on our trip, we came by the Longniddry Bents. The place had a nice beach, and was literally empty, perhaps because it had rained just a while ago, and was perfect for wild swimming. She used her purple scarf, that I liked very much, to enclose her modesty as she changed into her black backless bathing suit. I felt I was witnessing a rose transform into a plush female form. Or perhaps had seen a Selkie from the Norwegian folklore that transformed into a human form. I had a green hand towel that helped me change. It was obvious to me that she had done this kind of stuff before, as she was quicker than I was. As I folded my clothes and put them in place with my bag, I saw there was an elderly *couple behind us, sitting with their dog. She was already near the water, and smiling at me.*

"Maybe it wasn't such a good idea after all"*, she said as she checked the temperature of the sea water with her feet and hands. There were jellyfish floating around in the water, so we had to be careful. Seeing her in that suit, swimming in the shallow waters, reminded me of Kate Winslet from Little Children. I felt as if I was in a movie of my own, and that this was definitely the scene where I realized how much I wanted to touch her. While in the water, I would sometimes dip my hands under the surface with my palms cupped and pull out some water to throw on her body. This made her gasp and take a big gulp of air inside her lungs and turn her back on me as her eyelids stretched and shrunk, in a slow and graceful manner, like the leaves of Mimosa pudica, commonly known as the touch-me-not plant.*

Towards the end of the day, as always, I would escort her to her bike downstairs, and bid her goodnight, hiding my longing heart that hoped there would be an evening when she would be in my arms as I kissed her and whispered in her ears a midnight's dream.

Elpenor

O princess of the woodland sprites
you owe me a kiss in the rain
for I long without rest and hope beyond reason
to bear the weight of your soft moist lips on my lips
to behold the mimes of your laved lashes and lids
to drink the rain
infused with the scent of your sweet sweat
running as rivers from your temples
along the divine curves of your glowing face

O goddess of desires
I dream of you in a dream of the night
basking in the warmth of your nubile body
entangled and blent into mine
changing shapes as we morph and transform
like a burning flame dancing on the tip of a candle wick
exuding fumes of joy and gleaming with pleasure

fuelled with eternal exuberance and perpetual passion

O flower of the evening lilies
I seek your hand for a private dance
waltzing to the slow rhythm of shimmering stars and
flickering fireflies
under the blue velvet and the spotlight of the uncut
moon
with the melodies of your deepest breaths
and the summer winds
and the ballads of the heavy clouds
and the crashing waves
tip-toeing on the sands of time
twirling in the arms of life

O geist of an ephemeral beauty
let me sing my silent songs
let me breathe in life quietly
let me dream with open eyes
let me hold you without touch
let me transcend logic
let me love you unbound

We met not often in the common room of our office building. Her face would light up and her eyes would glow, gushing with a burst of tacit emotions and unvoiced desires left only to my imagination. Gifted to me albeit was a faint smile, veiling all that I longed for from me.

I was more poised and in control. I thought I was. Without the slightest changes in the contour of my facial muscles, I would just look at her and nod.

Our encounters were not always dull. Once we sat next to each other during an office seminar. The notion of sitting close to each other was enough for us to ditch the drudgery of pretending. We made up castles out of thin air and laughed at our silly jokes. For that small instance in time, we were lost in our own world. An imaginarium where the boundaries between us evaporated and our fake faces faded. The applauding audience at the end burst our impermanent bubble and woke us up to find ourselves trapped, bound, and helpless.

It was the weekly movie night at my friend's place, and I was slouching by the couch. Tess – a Roman Polanski romantic drama was the film on the CinemaScope. She came and sat beside me on the sofa and put her head on a cushion that pushed against my left shoulder. She had *been there the whole evening. We were both exhausted from our tiring hide-and-seek of emotions. I was out of words to wrap my feelings any further, and preferred the oblivion in silence. She must have mustered a lot of energy to try and keep up the conversation. She weaved in references to the beautiful countryside and the strong will of the peasant girl portrayed in the film. I would occasionally nod or give away colloquial tokens of acknowledgements. I had not realized how close she had drawn her face to mine through the course of the movie. Suddenly I heard her pause as if she was awaiting my reply. I asked her to repeat, a bit ashamed as my reluctant involvement was finally revealed. She put her lips on my left ear and whispered – "**Why don't you just say what you really want to say to me**".*

Appetite for love

By whom, as, as much as,
to be loved you love
is rare, ephemeral, incongruous, romantic
but I hope it's not too much an ask
for a soul that loved with all of heart
with all my heart I seek

One's capacity to give, and the appetite for love
rests on the age and size of one's heart
Your heart, I've seen, is as young as the moment that
defines the present
as deep as the oceans, as big as Jupiter, as vast as the
Milky Way
The depths of your love defy my imagination,
as I wish to live to see the day your heart truly opens up
to me

Every moment spent with you is a wish come true,
wishes that were broken,
wishes I had lost, ceded, forgotten

Every other day my body gave in to frustration
every other night my heart said linger on
just until tomorrow

She told me she wanted to show me something. I sensed a mystery in her voice and an unfamiliar shyness in her eyes, veiled by the mischievous light grin on her face. She asked me to meet her at the top of the hill one afternoon. I could recall my previous visits to the popular picnic spot on the hill, and expected nothing unseen to see there this time. Still, I did not want to take away her naivety. I rather preferred it over my logical but dreary judgment.

When I reached there, I saw she was already waiting underneath a tree with a basket of sandwiches and a bottle of wine laid on a checkered blanket. The red and white squares were in sync with her light-blue frock, exhibiting her as a beautifully wrapped Christmas present.

We chatted about tidbits of life and how time had treated us so far. After a while we started to saunter up the hill as our shadows grew with the ever so slanting sun in the sky. I stood at the top, with no higher cliff obtruding the vast vista of the valley.

At a mighty distance was a plane flying, gleaming in the orange sunlight, chalking a smoke trail in the clear and lifeless sky. Although it must be moving at sonic velocity, the distance between us made it look like an old lady taking a stroll in her tri-walker. The steam oozing high chimneys seemed like burning cigars. Spiking erect among the average sized buildings in the valley was the steeple of an old church. There was a sound floating in the air. It was coming from the carnival nearby. I could see the birds flying motionless with the cold and chilling breeze. The sun was sinking deeper and deeper in the hills, changing colours of the horizon from red to violet. Facing opposite to it was the moon, half way into its completion, waiting patiently to declare its reign over the night sky.

It was then that she grabbed my hand. I looked into her blue mesmeric eyes, trying to fathom the depths of the abysses, gazing at me with such overwhelming passion. Her lips had parted as she gasped slowly. I leaned in to feel the warmth of her breath. She gently closed her eyes and raised her face. It was loud and clear. It was a plea for liberty, an appeal for acknowledgement, an act of greed, an amorous expression, and a call for love. I felt my grip on her getting tighter. The red ribbon which held her golden hair waved in the air as if it were attached to a soaring kite. The smell on her neck smothered me and alleviated my focus on the material world. I felt the silky texture of her cheek as I grazed my hands against her reddened face. I kissed her.

The girl with a flying kiss

Winds to the land
that bear the cries of the sea
and quench the thirst that was long forgotten
and water the seed that lay dormant
crushed under weight
and burnt in heat

Like a newfound joy
the gentle touch of the first drops of rain
that reminds the dead grass
of its colour and its scent
the warmth of spring
and nourishing soil
that shapes the life
and brightens its fate

A serenade to my sorrows
a kiss to my wounds
a blanket for my cold nights
and an embrace to soothe

Is how my eyes, my lips,
my ears, and my skin
would hold locked in their memory
what your presence meant to me

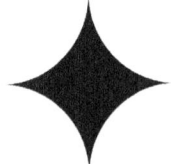

She went up to the night lamp and turned it on. Her body lit up sideways like an oak tree at sunset. Her towel lay lifeless at her feet like the leaves which bared the tree of all her diffidence in the wake of winter. The dim lights of the setting sun cast a profile of her curvy trunk. Her branches stretching out upwards in exhibition, as if begging to bargain her impeccable beauty for a humanly touch. I felt myself like the rising moon, overseeing this silent act of desire with oozing audacity, and knowing that mine would be the only light smothering her in the impending moments.

White Soul

In a curious dream on an August night
not so warm, not so cold
I saw a dame who sang to me
her tales of time, new and old

She said -
"Beyond the hills from far away lands
I followed the whimpers of lonely hearts"
Her feathered wings were weary and torn
hoodwinked and gulled by orcs ersatz

I spoke three words
in an aching voice
whispering to her
"Let me try"

I put her hands upon my chest
and saw a flame in her empty eyes
I tried to reach out as I broke my sleep
She was ebbing away on silver beams

I wandered in search of that lost white soul
tending to the matters of my longing heart
I looked at dew on the morning petals
and waved my hands at the dimming stars
As I held myself and ventured out
poised determined void of doubt
I searched the woods and combed the sea
reaching as far as far could be
arriving at last to my final rest
at a place that looked foreign at best

And I filled my senses until I could not take in any more
white clouds marching across the blasting white sky
white leaves waving on the branches of the
white trunks of silver shining trees
white birds flying over the glistering white water
white grass dancing on the bed of gold and green

Upon which my body lay uncoiled lost in your thoughts
as the cold clear water went past politely
pushed away by the unstrange Autumn breeze
that brushed the surface of the white lake
gently like a harp
with its familiar touch waking my body up
to the simple thought

It really is your breath that surrounds me
it really is your hair that grants me shelter
it really is your skin on my skin
holding my soul within your divine embrace
I realized - your love is the colour that brings my
shadows to life and the rhythm to my lonely heart.

PAIN

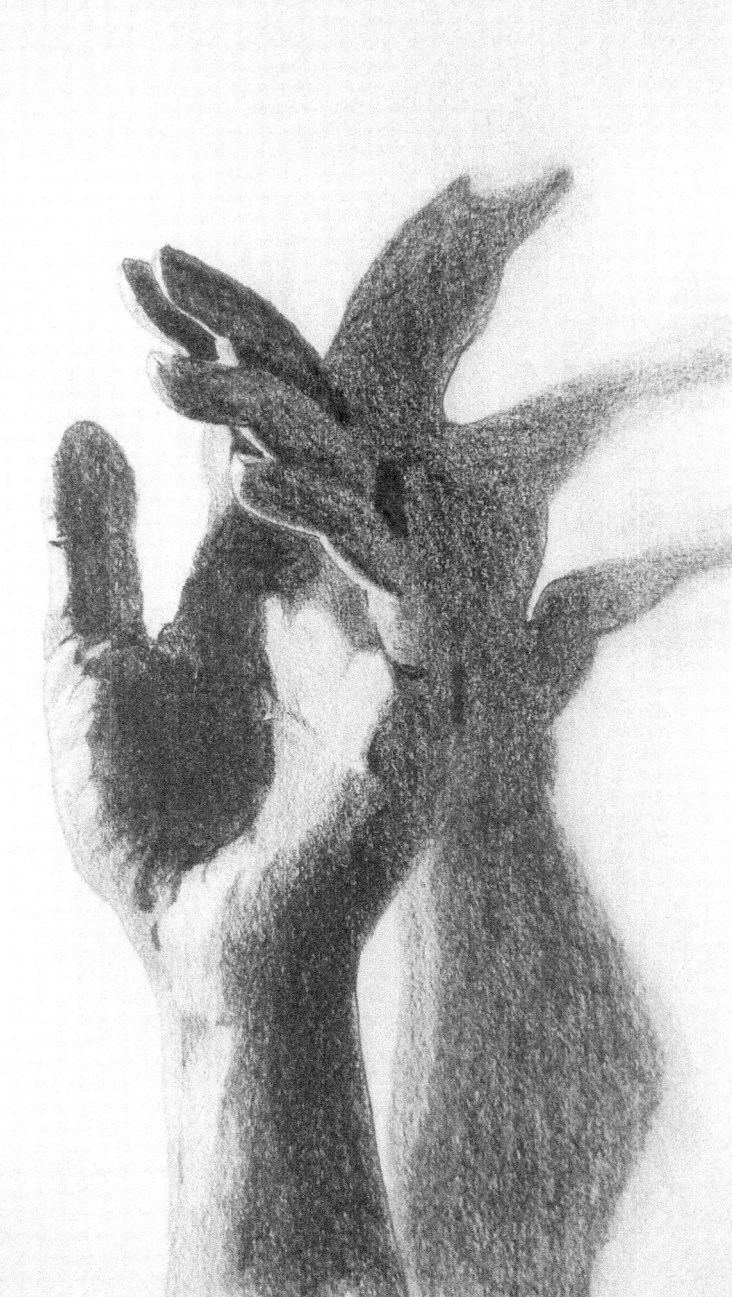

I hold on to the memories of our time spent together, remembering you every day just to keep you alive as long as I can, and to help me breathe too. With each day your face fades away a little and that's how I know my end is certain too.

A separation

I long for your warmth
in the brightening yellow of the dawn
I desire your company
under the blue and under the starry skies

I miss your presence
with every breath I take
I feel your touch
when I close my eyes
I search for your traces
in every soul that passes by
I think of reaching out
in every passing hour

To be as close to you
as thunder to the clouds
as stars to the night

as smell to the flowers
as colours to the rainbow
as beats to the heart
so that no moment is dropped for a photon of light that
travels between us

If you're a dream
I would forever keep my eyes unperturbed
If you're a lost soul
I'd search for you until my last breath

The moment that I behold your face for the last time
is not here yet,
and is tucked away deep into the future
This hope brings some peace to my restless heart
silently waiting for this separation of our souls to
evaporate

I wonder how many such tales of love are ill-fated and lost in oblivion, and yet how fertile is our undaunted imagination that incessantly bears the labour of this sacred feeling.

It is an enchantment that fills our hearts with an ocean of passion, and nurtures our soul to ascend the vastness of our existence.

The cycle of pain

Burnt, broken, beaten
you reaped no fruit but thorns from your trees
dreich dark winter of snow
not the green of spring
sickness plague rot
not health happiness glee

The hand you once held in hope
bit stung maimed left you to bleed
yet you fail to see
all that burns turns into the same grey
lifeless colourless frail
Accepting the darkness of your past
with all your heart
despite its tragedy and jolt
you deny the light of your future
sincere and pure

You fear getting hurt again
but not the looming ill fate
that you may not recognise a chance at true love
blooming in those ashes
and may deny such a bliss to you
and to the other burnt soul

Why must misdeeds of one lost soul
be burden for countless many more
why must this chain not break
why shouldn't love prevail

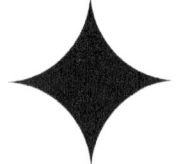

I rest
in the rhythmic lullabies
of the calm waters
in the company of
lowly waves that kiss
the shores gently
under the steady blue sky
with soft white clouds
that bring peace

I ride
along my two wheeled friend, Becky
with a prime joy within
and a secret scent of a woman on my mind

Thoughts of you

The pleasures of time spent together
the anticipation of what could be
entranced by affection
enduring the pain of hope
the thoughts of you
unthinkingly infiltrate my mind undisclosed

Escaping seamlessly into my unwary awareness
overloading my emotions
with an unhoped-for happiness
as if I were blinded
by staring incessantly
at the unfettered brightness of the mid-day sun
reducing my senses to only that of true love

In my misery I wonder
I know not how to learn not to miss you
so dearly, so often

Make haste, my darling
the scent of your love
is wearing off

Slow the clocks around
there's too much life
too many moments
within this moment
we must live them all

It's a miracle
what never could be
what lovers search in love
we have it all
between

But don't get hinged
upon the now
just savour, remember
the day
the sun would take over
tomorrow
won't be today

Unrequited

My rigid body convulsed
and ached with throes
and it burnt with sickening fever

My bruised heart grew heavy with solemn sorrow
my shrinking lungs choked with consuming fear
my unsettled mind numbed in grim despair
my poignant eyes drowned in deep tears

My weary soul refused to cross another unending hour
with this dreadful thought and its unbearable weight
treading closer to the day we may meet
to endorse a love unrequited

There is nothing more left for us to lose in our present, but perhaps things could be preserved and salvaged for our future. All we need is to shed the ineffectual aspects of our being, and be naked.

For, now, we can drop our weapons and guards as the war between us is over, and we can choose to be allies in the war that continues within. For there could now be peace between us, and perhaps, eventually, joy and happiness within too.

The man I used to be

I would try if I had the strength in me
but I'm not the man I used to be,
My smiles are all not simpers
a few are fawning gestures
a mask of maturity
a cloak of conformity
concealing my condition
from condoling contempting cowardly eyes

I would try if I had the strength in me
but I'm not the man I used to be,
I fail and I fear
there may not be much that's left of me
in my search for love that's yet to yield
to share my stories of brightest days,
the fragility of naked nights, and
the warmth of my cindering youth

I would try if I had the strength in me
but I'm not the man I used to be,
time ticks incessantly
slipping away through my ever clenching fists
as I watch in pain
in anger, in vain
my ageing and eroding grit

I would try if I had the strength in me
but I'm not the man I used to be,
those nights I have
alone when I cry
I would scream to be heard
but my voice doesn't matter
blue I am not for my sadness within
that lingers on, a loneliness it is

I feel I had just started learning to fly. Then my wings were cut within the first few seconds of my flight.

It seems as if I've lost the sense of my purpose in life, my clarity about what I want or need, and my understanding of what life has to offer.

Dawning dusk

Do candlewicks lose their thirst
and autumn leaves loathe heights
do stars go blind as they shoot around heavens
is no will preserved in melting ice

Bread and books lose in taste
as racing legs wander without exception
sight becomes insignificant
as eyes pervert observation

All that glitter lose their shine
in empty exhibitions
indentures to fathom mysteries
preparations become persecutions

Forgotten touch of kinsman skin
the ones I once adored

unfailingly failed to sense presence
neither nearby nor in lore

Blotches of bliss battered to nil
shades of sorrow festered and faded
from the canvas of life steadily and slowly
all colours of the heart decayed

A silence rackets by my quietude
sinking me inside
a dusk dawns upon my soul
paralysing life

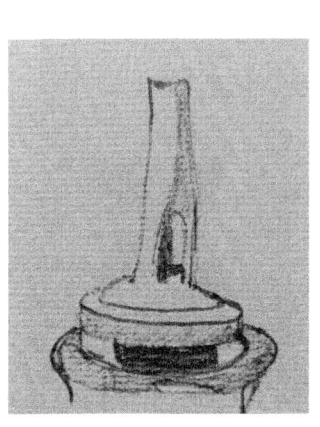

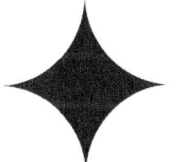

HOPE

I've lived long enough to have learnt that I can't let my expectations ruin my experiences.

If I could be someone I would look up to myself, it would be a measure of my contentment.

Aurora

Freshness of invigorating virgin brisk air
Inspires enlivens dawning life
Unveils undeniable simplicity
Blatant candid subtle smile

Tang a vista praise aroma amorous embrace
Pity 'tis oblivious to beauty concealed so certain

Whispering whimpers O wondering wanderer
Ice on cloaked water
Unfetter gush stream
Unfold extend fly
Hatch sprout flourish
Your perpetual fire

Beauty

I know not what it is
I know though it is

I could feel it in the splendour of the dawn
when the birds whisper their graceful song
Flying with the fresh tender aromatic breeze
under the purple-blue umbrella sky
patched in shades of red and orange.

I grasp its presence
in the allure of numbers and their modesty
in their enigma and simplicity
in their faculties and futility
in their hospitality and hostility

I admit its essence
in my breath and my undying quest

I see it playing as a child in my inner-garden
through my mind's window
and I find
it as the coachmen
carrying people in front of my eyes

So, my planned pursuit is but a wander in oblivion
I don't see smell touch taste nor hear
as mine is only the sense of beauty

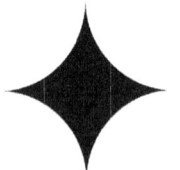

Choice of Dilemma

Why dodge simplicity
absorbed in the oddity of curiosity
abandoned forsaken
which lies in the silent wake of content

Invinced is the reality of this sleep
convinced is the dreamer behind closed eyes

Resolute is the state of time
undaunted despite desperate documenting
and photography

Silent are the plays
and the prose repetitive
oblivious to the obvious novelty

Unworthy and dull is the war
unjustified in the uncouth morality

This coloration of the canvas is perpetual
as is the cycle of the sun
so is the choice of dilemma
which too is a truth too simple

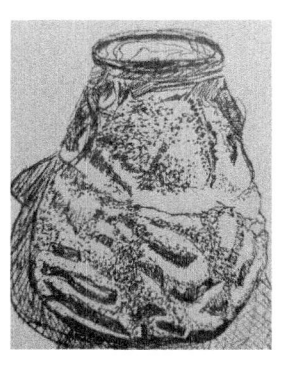

Unbroken

When you hold
what you feel
the chalice in your grip
is it fear or remorse
or something surreal

Do you contest the taste
of emptiness and loss
the inevitable truth
with every tick of your clock
the ship on the lake
that sank in quicksand
do you still see its mast
through the horizon of your hands

When you gaze upon the river
do you search for eternal flame

spent on the fireflies
in the chasing game

Through the lifeless winter
in your broken dreams
do you wish to shed the burden
and fill the craters within

The hope of a rainbow
in your wet searching eyes
brings the shining sun
across the colourless sky

Burden of a prayer

A wave gushes
pushes behind
amidst the clutches
of the wild and blind

Uprooting the sense of existence
is born this unnerving feeling
burning the bonds of riches
have I lost in limbs and in time

There's no just
nor more of divine
a field of dust
and an unnamed shrine

Of raptured beauty
and captured souls

no integrity
the shadows behold

A flower blooms
in the looming sight
praying for rain
reaching out for light

Bewildered wisdom

Where nests the bird
whose flight was freedom
that once flew in sight
in the wide blue yonder

The horizon blinks closer
as I stand ever tall
but the freshness in air
seems forgotten and lost

The wrath is unleashed
of untamed time
unravelling the mysteries
of a frozen mind

Burrowed I find
the strength uncast

flowing through veins
of my throbbing heart

The kite of ambition
is soaring again
as droplets of water
drizzling in rain

Bewildered yet alive
this wisdom I gained
I cannot be stopped
I cannot be chained

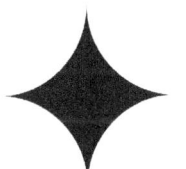

अहसास

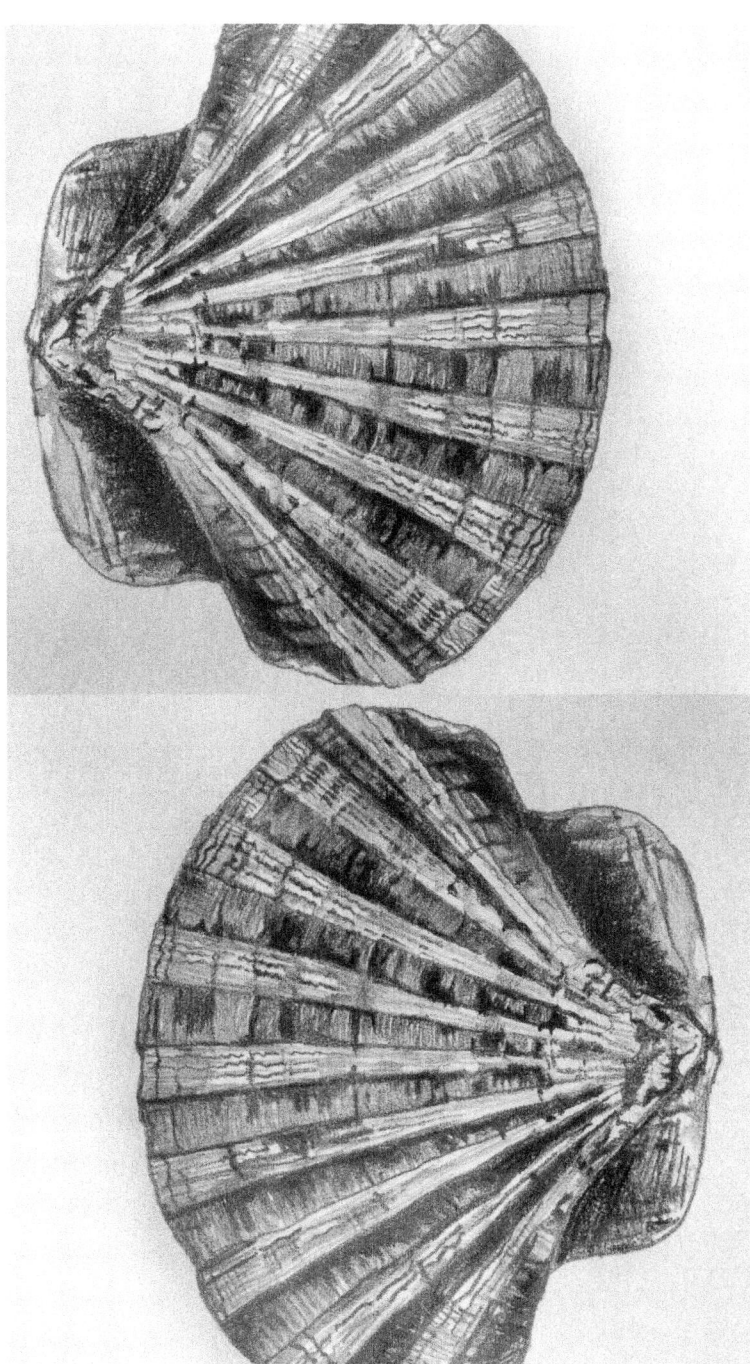

ख़्वाहिश कुछ ऐसी है
के हर ख़्वाहिश ना हो पूरी
बाकी हो ख़्वाहिश ऐसी भी
जो साँसें लेने दे

राह की चाह

सफर मुकद्दर मंजिलों का
लोग कहते जिंदगी है
पर परछाइयाँ शीश महल में
दिखती मुझको जिंदगी है

चांदनी में डूबा सरोवर
प्रेमवश नम की रात में
बावरे भवरे हुए
खुश्क फूलों की छांव में

फट पड़ी धर्ती भी आखिर
झेल धूप की उष्णता को
उजड़े जड़ भी उतरे रंग भी
बनके खाक सब पतझड़ में

जो खत्म हुआ वह इंसान था
नगमा तो बस अंतराल पर है
गुमशुदा गर्दिश मौजों का
मुकाम हर मझधार पर है

ख़्वाहिश-ए-मोहब्बत

मिले सदक़े में भी नहीं उसकी सदाक़त
जो फ़क़ीर बन फ़रियाद करूं
न मिट्टी में है ख़ुशबू छुपी उसकी
जो मूरत में उसको तराश लूँ
मौजूद नहीं फ़िज़ा में वो
के भर लूं अपनी सांसों में
बस फ़िक्र है अब बाक़ी इन
ग़म भरी आँखों में
उसके आग़ाज़ की तसल्ली नहीं शामिल
किसी भी ख़याल में
इक ख़याल ही लिख दे कभी कोई
के हो कुछ उम्मीद का अक़ीदा
इन फ़िज़ूल ख़र्च हो चुकीं
मेरी ख़्वाहिशों में

अभी अभी

ना समझ मुझे काफ़िर आवारा
ना ख़ुद को जान मासूम परी
आँखें तो टकराईं पहले भी
इश्क़ हुआ पर अभी अभी

होलियाँ खेलीं हमने
है रंग चढ़ा पर अभी अभी
नज़ारे हज़ारों हमने देखे
है चाह बनी पर अभी अभी

इस मौसम में मचल जाने दो
बरसात रुकी है अभी अभी
कुछ देर ख़ुशी को बढ़ जाने दो
मुस्कान मिली है अभी अभी

अपनी ज़िद को थोड़ा छोड़ो
इस वक्त को ना गुज़र जाने दो
बात को पूरी हो जाने दो
बात बनी है अभी अभी

महफ़िलें तो काफ़ी मिलीं
पर साथ मिला है अभी अभी
जो छोड़ गए तुम मुझे अकेला
राह में यूँ ही चलने को
ग़म तो पहले भी हुआ है
दिल टूटेगा अभी अभी

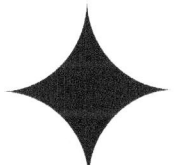

गिला-ए-अहद

अगर रूह है रौशनी
क्यूँ लगता के वो कैद है
क्यूँ ख़ाली सी हैं साँसें
जो गुलज़ार जिंदगी है

हर लम्हे में अगर आलम है
हर लम्हा क्यूँ इंतज़ार है
'गर सफर है बेहतर मंजिल से
क्यूँ राह में ग़म बरकरार है

ख़ामोश अकेली रातों में
मासूम थका दिल यूँ ही पूछे
कितनी वो नज़रें बाकी हैं
जिनसे जुदाई बाकी है

हं ही ग़मगीन क्यूँ रहते हैं
इतनी शिद्दत क्यूँ करते हैं
क्या दौर ही वो गुज़र गया
जब और भी आशिक़ होते थे

ख़बर

अक्सर यूँ हाल ना पूछ मेरा
यूँ हाल बुरा हो जायेगा
इतने प्यार की आदत नहीं
है प्यार मुझे हो जायेगा

कोई कशिश है तुझको भी
इतनी जो फ़िक्र है हो जाती
इस हर मर्ज़ की झिक झिक में
है याद किसी की कब आती

हैं ख़ुश हो लेते बस इस पर ही
कि शायद सेहर की आस है
के ग़म ना हो जो खुल जाये
ये राज़ अभी भी राज़ है

तो ना पूछ मुझे क्या चाहता हूँ
ना पूछ किसका मलाल है
बस पूछ ले हाल मेरा मुझसे
इस पूछ की मुझे फिराक है

फिर डरता हूँ इस बात से भी
दिल यूँ ही गुम हो जायेगा
अक्सर यूँ हाल ना पूछ मेरा
यूँ हाल बुरा हो जायेगा
इतने प्यार की आदत नहीं
है प्यार मुझे हो जायेगा

भूतावास

कहने को जग मुट्ठी में है
हर देश बगल की बात है
फिर भी जो बगल में हैं मेरे
कभी देते नहीं पयाम हैं
इस नए पन की आड़ में
ये कैसा कारावास है
हैं रहते यहां अब लोग नहीं
यहां होता भूतावास है

रफ्तार से जीने की इस लत में
जीना ही हम क्या भूल गए
अनित्य संवेगशीलता में
सब की खुशबू भूल गए
यादें बुनना रिश्ते रखना
भूतों का कहां अंदाज़ है

हैं रहते यहां अब लोग नहीं
यहां होता भूतावास है

मन को छूकर हंस देते हैं
मौजों में खेल लेते हैं
पहचान कहां इनकी आसान
मुझ जैसे ही ये दिखते हैं
रो देती है रूह भी मेरी
जब खाली फैले हाथों में
फिर दिल लेकर
सपने लेकर आंखों में नए
नए राही को सलाम करते हैं
अधूरे अफसानों को लेकर
नई कविताएं रचते हैं
दो पल की मुलाकातों से
जन्मों के नाते रखते हैं
वो लोग कहां अब मिलते हैं
मिलते हैं कुछ यारों से जब
भूतों की चर्चा करते हैं
हैं रहते यहां अब लोग नहीं
यहां होता भूतावास है

मुझ एक दिल इंसान को
इन गूंगे फीके वादों ने
टूटी बिखरी हसरतों को
लेकर चलना सिखा दिया
सच्चा दिल सुलझा मन
अब नहीं दिखता सर-ए-आम है

इस नए पन की आड़ में
ये कैसा कारावास है
हैं रहते यहां अब लोग नहीं
यहां होता भूतावास है

इल्ज़ाम-ए-इश्क

हम शिकवा क्या करें
वो मौसम ही ना आया
आरज़ू बस इतनी है
कुछ रुक कर गुज़रे जिंदगी

अफसोस क्या करें
ना था पाया जो गंवाया
वो मेरी ख्वाहिश ही ना बने
है किस्मत जो गैर की

आँहें ही क्या भरें
है गम भी ये पराया
कभी यादों में ना रहूं उनकी
जिन्हें आता है भुलाना

हम उफ भी क्यों करें
ये ठोकर ही है नकली
इश्क हो तो हद ही पार हो ऐसे
के गम में भी आए मज़ा

हम इश्क क्या करें
इस नादान ज़माने में
वो लोग नहीं मिलते
जिन्हें आता है इश्क करना

फकीर-ए-इश्क

ये दिल नहीं चाहता
मुश्किलें आसान करना
थोड़ा सुकून जरूर होगा
'गर दिख जाए मंजिल

बेशक कम हैं वो लोग जिन्हें
पहला ही इश्क गवारा है
हमनें तो हर बाज़ी खोई
हर इश्क अकेले चाहा है

गुस्ताख़ हंसीं नहीं हैं हम
खूबी हममें है थोड़ी कम
दिल देखोगे पर गौर से जब
दिख भीड़ में जाएंगे हम

शायर तो यूं ही हैं हम
'गर मिट गए अकेलेपन में
कहलाएंगे शहीद
इश्क के मैदान-ए-जंग में

दुआ नहीं करता रब से
मोहब्बत पाने की
दुआ करता हूं दिल से तह-ए अपने
मैं उस जमाने की
हर इश्क के बदले इश्क मिले
इश्क की बारिश हो
फकीर-ए-इश्क नां बन्ना पडे
किसी भी शायर को

तक़दीर-ए-इश्क़

मुहब्बत इतनी भी ना मिली हमें
उस पत्थर बेवफा से
के चर्चे में उसके उसे
कभी साबिक़ भी कह सकें हम
जुड़ जुड़ कर बार बार मेरा
दिल इतनी बार टूटा
के इश्क़ में बद्नसीबी की
मिसाल बन गए हम

उम्मीद नहीं छोड़ी उसके
किसी भी झूठे वादे की
चाहे यकीं करके ख़ुदसे
कितना ही उलझे हम
दफ़्न हुईं बेमौत जवां
इस दिल की ख़्वाहिशें इतनीं

के अधूरी हसरतों का
क़ब्रिस्तान बन गए हम

इश्तिहा की आग में उसकी
इस्मत अपनी झोंक दी
अपनी शहवतों को
सादेपन में छुपा दिया
लूट लूट कर बार बार उसकी
जिस्मी दिनायतों में
अपनेपन के सौदेबाज़ी में
बाज़ार-ए-हुस्न बन गए हम

मुड़ कर भी नहीं देखा उसने
उस रात इन रोती आँखों में
दिल हाँथ पर रख कर, गिड़ गिड़ा कर
चाहे जितना चीखे हम
गिर गिर कर कागजों पर
ये आँसूं इतनी बार फूटे
गिले शिकवों के अल्फ़ाज़ में
कच्चे शायर बन गए हम

अकेलापन

जिस दिशा में पड़ जाएं नजरें
बस गैर अनजान सड़कें हैं
अजनबी चेहरे अंकही बातें
अनाम हवा अंजान मौसम है

कोई लक्ष्य नहीं इन क़दमों का
हूँ कहाँ में ये भी पता नहीं
वो नशा भी अब अंजान सा है
जिससे थी ये रफ़्तार मिली

क्या कुछ पाया क्या कुछ खोया
हासिल है हुआ क्या पता नहीं
मांगी थी नहीं मैंने रब से
ऐसे जीने की दुआ कभी

किसी पल को थमने नहीं देता
ये वक्त भी मेरा नहीं साथी
जिस हाल में हो जीवन चाहे
है उम्र ये बस बढ़ती जाती

वो लोग नहीं हैं आस पास
हों जिनसे बातें मन की
इस अडग अकेलेपन में
महफ़ूज़ नहीं पहचान अपनी

है नहीं पता क्या कल होगा
होली होगी या रण होगा
क्या निखरेंगें रंग फूलों पर
या मातम सा समा होगा
पर सपना इक आँखों में है
हसरत है इक दिल की मन की
जाऊं जब इस जहान से मैं
दो आँखें हों भीगीं नम सी

Printed in Great Britain
by Amazon